Edward Gorey
Plays
Cape Cod

Puppets, People, Places, & Plots

by Carol Verburg

www.Boom-Books.com

For everybody who helped
starting with the FOE
ending with the EGH&M
with gratitude, especially to Edward,
for all the fun we had

ISBN: 978-0-9834355-1-8

Cover design by Barbara Oplinger   www.boplinger.com

Front cover photo and interior photos by Carol Verburg

Back cover photo by Alex Bedrosian

Contents

Some Comments from the Press

"Given the subject matter of his books – a child abducted and sacrificed to an Insect God, a family stuck with a hairy, penguinlike houseguest who won't leave – it should come as no surprise that Gorey takes to the footlights on little bat's wings. Gorey's stage work has the same air of impromptu surreality as his books; his scripts are stripped-down, deadpan sendups of Victorian conventions, from damsel-in-distress melodramas and moralistic children's tales to pornography. Those who like their gloom elegant and with a dash of Dada treasure Gorey's eccentric sensibility."

– Bill Marx, *The Boston Globe*, Monday, September 2, 1996

"Those who have read any of Gorey's 75 small books have no doubt asked what on earth this man is trying to say or do. . . . One might speculate that Gorey is trying to make a deep commentary on life or to frighten the reader. One might ask how serious is he about this murder and melodrama. These speculations are put soundly to rest after viewing *Useful Urns*, which is basically about futility, triviality and fun. The plots are anything but introspective. They move from flirtation, to sex, to murder, to death and other highly entertaining actions in a matter of minutes. Gorey does not take any of these actions seriously. He takes nothing seriously. Even that emptiness, often mulled over deeply in theater, is not taken seriously."

– K.C. Myers, *The Advocate*, Thursday, July 5, 1990

"Less than 5 minutes into the second performance of *Inverted Commas* . . . the lights flickered, the air conditioners fizzled and the power went out, plunging the teeny theater into darkness and unbearable discomfort.

"It was a good sign.

"Gorey's work is so infested with hapless creatures, murderous children, eccentric characters and unexplainable insanity that the electrical mishap was just the thing needed to set the mood."

– Alan W. Petrucelli, *The Cape Cod Times*, Monday, July 10, 1995

"Written, Directed, and Designed by Edward Gorey"

A noteworthy, if erratic, event in certain Cape Cod households during the 1990s was the arrival of an intricately drawn black-and-white postcard announcing "An Entertainment by Edward Gorey." The upcoming production might be a revue, a play, or a puppet show. To see it, one might have to find a former bowling alley in Provincetown, a converted convenience store in Bourne, a tent in Dennis, or a rehabbed mechanics' garage in Cotuit. Each script came fresh off the manual typewriter of the Cape's most notorious recluse, the artist and author known for his grimly funny little books, his Tony-award-winning costumes and sets for *Dracula,* and his opening credits for PBS's *Mystery.* As the postcard hit the mailboxes, he was likely to be swearing to me over lunch at Jack's Outback that he would never, never set foot in a theatre again. Fortunately the labor pains of rehearsal, like those of childbirth, fade from memory once the opus meets the public.

This is a brief and very personal chronicle of my decade producing, stage-managing, publicizing, and for that matter instigating almost all of Edward Gorey's original theatrical productions. As well as creative collaborators, Edward and I were friends and neighbors in the Cape Cod village of Yarmouthport. We spent a good deal of time together: saw plays and movies, lunched, dined, talked about everything, traded interests (he gave me *Buffy the Vampire Slayer* and *The X-Files*; I gave him *The Invention of Love* and Morphine), and frequently drove each other to distraction. From the theatre standpoint, our greatest mutual gift was wholehearted support. We made each other's work, AKA play, possible.

Only enough biography is included here to illuminate that work. If you wonder what Edward Gorey's life on Cape Cod was like, I recommend my mystery *Croaked,* which began as one of our *idées du jour* over lunch. His scripts will be published soon, too. My main aim for now (as when he lived) is to connect his theatrical visions with an appreciative audience.

Edward Gorey's Theatrical
(created, designed, & directed

The White Canoe: an Opera Seria for Hand Puppets
(music by Daniel Wolf; dir. Carol Verburg)
Cotuit Center for the Arts
at Freedom Hall, Cotuit   September 1 - 23, 2000

Papa Was a Rolling Stone: a Christmas Story
(coauthored with Carol Verburg; dir. Joe Richards)
Cotuit Center for the Arts   December 3 - 19, 1999

Moderate Seaweed
outdoor benefit for Cotuit Center for the Arts   August 28, 1999

English Soup
Cotuit Center for the Arts   October 2 - 25 1998
Storyopolis, Los Angeles   October 30 - 31, 1998

Omlet: or, Poopies Dallying and Rune lousse, rune de leglets: ou, sirence de glenouirres (puppets)
Cape Museum of Fine Arts, Dennis   July 25-26, August 8-9, 1998

Epistolary Play
Cotuit Center for the Arts   July 25 -August 30, 1997

Cautionary Tales (by Hilaire Belloc; puppets)
Cotuit Center for the Arts   October 26 - November 3, 1996

Heads Will Roll & Wallpaper
Theater on the Bay, Bourne   August 15 - September 7, 1996

Heads Will Roll (puppets)
MBL Club, Woods Hole   July 18-19, 1996
The Heron Bistro, Sandwich   June 1996

Entertainments on Cape Cod
by himself except as noted)

Stumbling Christmas
Theater on the Bay   November 24 - December 17, 1995
Pepper's Cafe, Hyannis   December 7, 14, & 21, 1995

Inverted Commas
Theater on the Bay   July 6 - 29, 1995

Salome (by Oscar Wilde) with the puppet curtain-raiser
Six Who Pass While the Lentils Boil (by Stewart Walker)
Theater on the Bay   February 3 - 19, 1995

Chinese Gossip
Theater on the Bay   July 21 - August 13, 1994

Blithering Christmas
Theater on the Bay   December 3 - 19, 1992

Crazed Teacups
Provincetown Theatre Company   July 23 - August 9, 1992

Flapping Ankles
Provincetown Theatre Company   July 18 - August 4, 1991

Stuffed Elephants
Woods Hole Theatre Company   August 17 - Sept. 2 , 1990

Useful Urns
Provincetown Theatre Company   June 28 - August 19, 1990

Lost Shoelaces (dir. Genie Stevens)
Magical Oysters Theatre Company
at Woods Hole Theatre Company   August 1987

Stage I: Cambridge

Although he shuddered to think of it, Edward Gorey's theatrical career spanned half a century. On the affinity level it probably started with his youthful interest in the ballet in Chicago. On the practical level, he launched it with the Poets' Theatre in Cambridge, Massachusetts, after World War II. Having finished his tour in the Army, as a clerk at Dugway Proving Ground in Utah, Ted Gorey went to Harvard University (where he had been accepted before the war) on the G.I. Bill. He and his roommate, Frank O'Hara, and an extraordinary group of friends–V.R. (Violet) "Bunny" Lang, John Ashbery, Alison Lurie, and John Ciardi, among others–scraped together a variety of theatrical pieces which they staged wherever they could and however their whimsy moved them. According to Edward, everybody in the Poets' Theatre did everything: write, direct, design, perform. Whenever he dipped into theatre after that, he approached it with the same light-hearted curiosity and open-mindedness.

Stage II: New York

Edward's next theatrical debut came three decades later. By then he was living in New York City and summering at his family's house in Barnstable on Cape Cod. In 1977, Stephen Currens adapted a number of Edward's books into *Gorey Stories*, with music by David Aldrich. Directed by Tony Tanner for WPA Theatre, this "comedy revue" (as *The New York Times* called it) was the first full-length staged version of his work. Edward participated when called on, but otherwise stayed out of the way. He did step in as designer when the full production of *Gorey Stories* opened the next year on Broadway, the night before Halloween. Although his costume and set designs for Frank Langella's *Dracula* were sending lucrative shivers through Manhattan, *Gorey Stories* collided with the New York newspaper strike and closed immediately. It resurfaced in the summer of 1980 at the Barnstable Comedy Club, followed by *More Gorey Stories* the next summer. Revived in Los Angeles in 1991, and here and there since then, *Gorey Stories* is his most often produced script.

The challenge of translating Edward's distinctive vision into theatre has continued, like the Sword in the Stone, to attract aspirants. *Tinned Lettuce, or The New Musical* came next. Edward himself took a more active role this time, choosing the title, designing the set and costumes, pruning the script, and working with director Daniel Levans to select the verses set to music by *Gorey Stories* composer Aldrich. A student cast of 19 performed the show at NYU's Tisch School of the Arts Department of Undergraduate Drama in 1985. *Amphigorey: The Musical* would follow in 1991, staged and again directed by Levans with a script created by producer/actor Kevin McDermott. The composer was Peter Golub; the sets were based on Gorey drawings. *Amphigorey* debuted at the American Musical Theatre Festival in Philadelphia, visited the Harvard-affiliated American Repertory Theatre, and then settled into New York's off-Broadway Perry Street Theatre. In the summer of 1999 a revamped version, with new music by Peter Matz and the title *Amphoragorey*, played at the Provincetown Repertory Theatre on Cape Cod. With new sets by Jesse Poleshuck and yet another new title, *The Gorey Details*, it opened at New York's Century Center for the Performing Arts on October 16, 2000.

Stage III: Cape Cod

After George Balanchine died in 1983, so did Edward's passion for the New York City Ballet. Within three years he moved full time to Cape Cod–into his own house, a rambling Greek Revival beauty on the Yarmouthport town green he'd bought with his *Dracula* earnings. (He accidentally left behind a mummified head which threw his Manhattan building into a tizzy, but that's another story.) Well known by now, he started introducing himself–or not demurring when he was introduced –as Edward rather than Ted. He didn't like Ed.

Not long after becoming a Cape resident, Edward saw a riveting pro-duction of Caryl Churchill's *Top Girls* at the Woods Hole Theatre Company. He tracked down director Genie Stevens and asked if she might want to direct something of his. She did, and he created *Lost Shoelaces.* It was staged in August 1987 by the Magical Oysters Theatre

PROVINCETOWN REPERTORY THEATRE PRESENTS
A MUSICAL ENTERTAINMENT
STORIES BY EDWARD GOREY MUSIC BY PETER MATZ
DIRECTION AND STAGING BY DANIEL LEVANS

Company under the aegis of the Woods Hole Theatre Company; parts of it were later performed for the Creative Club of Boston's Christmas dinner and auction. The eight cast members included *Top Girls* star Cathy Smith, Joe Richards, Vincent Myette, and Eric Edwards, who became Edward's core actors on the Upper Cape for the next decade.

Lost Shoelaces was the first entertainment to use both live actors and the troupe of handmade puppets Edward called Le Théâtricule Stoïque. Like *Tinned Lettuce*, the script was assembled from his published and unpublished writing, augmented with new pieces he wrote for the occasion. The previously unstaged parts in particular, as well as the show's organization, display a theatrical sensibility more illuminated by Dada, Beckett, and Japanese art (among others) than by the traditional concerns of accessibility and structure that have shaped most other people's stagings of his work.

I met Edward in 1988, at my first play on Cape Cod. This was a workshop benefit performance for the Barnstable Comedy Club of Kurt Vonnegut's *Cat's Cradle*, which I had adapted and codirected (with George McConville) in honor of the novel's 25th anniversary and the author's ties with the Club. My sister Bonnie, then an editor at Harcourt Brace, came to Cape Cod to discuss a book contract with Edward and brought him to the show. Afterward we crossed the street to the Barnstable Tavern, where we had a fine time talking and drinking till the bar closed. I hadn't seen *Lost Shoelaces*, but I liked Edward enormously and knew that sometime, somehow, I wanted to work with him.

The Community Hall in Woods Hole seats about a hundred, and it filled up for the short run of *Lost Shoelaces*. In 1990 the Woods Hole Theatre Company asked Edward to do another summer show. He supplied *Stuffed Elephants*. When I heard about it, I asked him if the production could travel for a few weekends to the Provincetown Theatre Company, where I was board president and part of the Playwrights' Workshop (now Lab). Edward said he would rather create a new show for the PTC.

We had a planning meeting at my house in Yarmouthport with a New York-based director who'd just finished a very successful play in Provincetown and was eager to tackle a Gorey piece. Also present was PTC cofounder Ray Martan Wells, older than Edward and no less formidable. Ray ended the discussion by telling Edward: "Of course you must direct it!" And so he did–directed and designed *Useful Urns* and *Stuffed Elephants* and most subsequent productions of his scripts on Cape Cod.

Crescendo

Edward created, and I produced, three entertainments with PAPA/PTC
(the Provincetown Academy of Performing Arts / Provincetown Theatre
Company) in three consecutive summers: *Useful Urns, Flapping Ankles,*
and *Crazed Teacups.* By 1992, the two-hour round-trip commute through
heavy summer traffic was getting to us. We shifted to the opposite end
of Cape Cod: Theater on the Bay in Bourne, where I'd been asked to
become artistic director and Edward's next six productions were staged.

TOB was the site of several firsts. *Blithering Christmas* was the first script
Edward wrote as a full-length play rather than assembled from old and
new work into an entertainment. *Salome,* by Oscar Wilde, was his first
shot at directing a play he didn't write. His first all-puppet show (aside
from human narrators) was *Heads Will Roll.* And his first Cape Cod productions that traveled were *Heads Will Roll,* reprised at the MBL Club in
Woods Hole, and *Stumbling Christmas,* at Pepper's Cafe in Hyannis.

1995 was a banner year: Edward directed *Salome* in February, *Inverted
Commas* in July, and *Stumbling Christmas* (Part 2 of an intended Christmas
trilogy) in December. *Chinese Gossip* and *Inverted Commas* reestablished
his custom of creating a new entertainment every summer. The third
show in that sequence was to have been *Tragic Secrets,* but a last-minute
injury to an actor forced us to cancel it. Instead we remounted *Heads
Will Roll* along with *Wallpaper,* the longest, most narrative piece from
Tragic Secrets. Edward himself stepped in as the Telegraph Boy, looking
like a gawky, white-bearded Boy Scout in his khaki shorts and sneakers,
and nervously checking his lines on the telegram he carried. He got
rave reviews for his bone-dry delivery, despite his fellow actors' endless
efforts to crack him up.

Edward often embedded private jokes in his scripts. Only ten years later
did *Wallpaper* yield up a secret. On encountering its heroine, her late
great-aunt tries to recall her name: "Freda? Fiona? Flora? Fidelma?
Fenella?" We knew no Fidelmas, but Edward did: New York City Ballet
patron Lincoln Kirstein's wife, a former designer of wallpaper.

THEATER ON THE BAY presents,
preceded by a puppet production of
SIX WHO PASS WHILE THE LENTILS BOIL
by Stewart Walker,

OSCAR WILDE'S
SALOME

Designed
and directed by
EDWARD GOREY

Music by
STRAVINSKY
and STRAUSS

Friday & Saturday at 8PM, Sunday at 5:30 PM
February 3-5, 10-12, 17-19, 1995
Trading Post Corners, Monument Beach (Bourne)
MA
Tickets $10   Reservations (508) 759-0977

During *Heads Will Roll* and *Wallpaper*, Edward and I were invited to do a show at the Cotuit Center for the Arts. We went over to talk with board president John Cira and executive director James Wolf and to look at the space. Edward and Jamie immediately got into a long, enthusiastic discussion about lithography. The arts center itself was a refurbished mechanics' garage with a garden out back which had recently–literally –been hit by a hurricane. Edward loved it, and we decided to jump right in with a Halloween production. The first of the half-dozen shows he would create in Cotuit was a puppet version of the book he was then illustrating, Hilaire Belloc's *Cautionary Tales*.

The next Spring I directed *Hamlet*; for that, Edward designed the poster and sets. He measured each section of the building's interior, set up the scale, and drew vaguely castle-like walls of black-and-white stones, finials, and drapes, most about four inches square, with gridded over-lays. Other artists from the Center gridded panels cut to fit the building's actual walls, and painted on Edward's blown-up drawings.

Hamlet being the first full-length play ever staged at the Arts Center, we had to make or borrow every item in it. Edward masterminded the costume plan, mainly by vetoing every piece of clothing I brought in that didn't match his vision of how the production should look. His ideal was burlap; we settled on velvets and golds. Casting began with

our usual core actors: Vincent Myette as Hamlet, Joe Richards as
Claudius, Eric Edwards as Polonius.

Meanwhile Edward wrote, and in July directed, *Epistolary Play*. This
series of letters read aloud by two actors had been inspired by the
mind-boggling success of *Love Letters*, in which I'd directed Edward's
regular actors Cathy Smith and Jane Macdonald, taking turns with my
recent Rosencrantz (and our lighting designer) Bill Ring. Edward's
version of a simple, portable, go-everywhere play called for his two
actors to play sixteen characters. But who could resist an *idée du jour*
that began life over lunch at Jack's Outback with the working title "The
Love Letters of Irma Vep"?

Edward's other response to *Hamlet* was *Omlet*, half of a benefit production he supplied the next summer for the Cape Museum of Fine Arts. I
had adapted my *Hamlet* script from several versions, including the
so-called Bad Quarto, a name Edward adored and incorporated into a
puppet skit involving a naughty dog. *Omlet* comprised his favorite
nonsensical bits of early pirate *Hamlets*. Staged in a festive outdoor tent,
the production had no live actors, only Le Théâtricule Stoïque.

The Cape Museum of Fine Arts presents

AN ETCETERIST ENTERTAINMENT

Devised by Edward Gorey for the puppets of Le Théâtricule stoïque in

MLET: OR,
POOPIES &
DALLYING
by Sir Francis Bacon

UNE LOUSSE ;
RUNE DE LEGLETS :
OU, SIRENCE DE
GLENOUIRRES
by Adelwyd Ogle

Sat & Sun afternoon at 4
July 25-26, August 8-9, 1998

Cape Museum of Fine Arts, Route 6A, Dennis Village, on the grounds of the Cape Playhouse
Admission $5 to performance and gallery exhibition of work by Edward Gorey
and Helen Pond & Herbert Senn

The second piece on the bill was *Rune Lousse, Rune de Leglets,* Edward's nonmusical parody of *Madame Butterfly* (and the stereotypes in it). He narrated the whole performance himself, reading his script from a stool beside the six-by-eight-foot puppet screen in his usual dry monotone.

Most of the late *Tragic Secrets* reappeared that October in *English Soup.* This was Edward's first production to travel off Cape: Storyopolis, a children's bookstore and art gallery in Los Angeles, flew the cast and crew out for Halloween weekend. Edward himself, who hadn't seen California since his Army leaves in the 1940s, predictably refused to go. His excuse was that he had to attend a Halloween staged reading of some of his previously performed pieces, directed by his friend Bobby Rosser, at the Cape Cod Repertory Theatre in Brewster. (Called *Drat!,* it would be followed by *Eek!* in 1999 and *Hist!* in 2000.) But Edward had refused every invitation involving airplane travel since his one and only trip abroad, to the Hebrides, decades earlier. He'd enjoyed it so much, he told me, that if he'd seen any land for sale he'd have stayed forever.

Decrescendo

By the late '90s, Edward's fascination with theatre was flagging. I had started spending winters in San Francisco; although we still talked frequently by phone, it wasn't the same as conferring in person every other day or so, airing the *idée du jour* over lunch or a movie. Besides, he said, he didn't see what more he could learn from creating shows on Cape Cod. He had already answered most of his theatrical questions, including how it would feel to appear onstage himself. He had tried making a video (of *Cautionary Tales,* with videographer Chris Seufert) and quit; nor did TV animation hold his interest.

The next summer Edward started work on his annual entertainment but didn't finish it. In August he did supply a short piece for puppets and narrators, *Moderate Seaweed,* to a benefit for the Cotuit Center for the Arts. He wanted to do another Christmas show, and over our now-daily summer lunches he tossed around ideas for adapting *The Haunted Tea Cozy,* his book version of *A Christmas Carol.* But after I left again for

California, he gave it up. The Arts Center substituted a one-act play Edward and I had created a few years earlier but not produced: *Papa Was a Rolling Stone: A Christmas Story.*

The last piece of writing Edward completed for the stage was the libretto for *The White Canoe: an Opera Seria for Hand Puppets.* This little gem was sparked by a 1999 letter from composer Daniel Wolf, then in Frankfurt, Germany, asking if Edward had ever considered doing some kind of musical theatre with his puppets. Edward responded with a stage adaptation of a long narrative poem he claimed every schoolchild once had to know, Thomas Moore's "The Lake of the Dismal Swamp":

> *They made her a grave too cold and damp*
> *For a soul so warm and true;*
> *And she's gone to the Lake of the Dismal Swamp,*
> *Where all night long, by a firefly lamp,*
> *She paddles her white canoe.*

During the night of April 6, 2000, the Cotuit Center for the Arts burned to the ground in a freak chimney fire. Less than a week later, on April 12, Edward had a heart attack. While his oldest friend, Consuelo Joerns, hurried over from Martha's Vineyard, I caught the first plane out of San Francisco, to sit by his hospital bed talking and reading (from *The Tale of Genji*, his favorite book), trying to lure him back from his coma. Edward left life moments after I left for dinner at his friend Rick Jones's house on Saturday, April 15.

My Yarmouthport house still had its winter tenants, and Edward's cats and belongings needed looking after, so at the request of his executors, I moved into his house. A horrified phone call came from Dan Wolf, now in Hungary: he'd just heard the bad news, days after completing the score for *The White Canoe.* What to do? Dan sent over the finished 45-minute opera, and I rounded up the cast Edward had written it for. I spent that grim summer rehearsing with Le Théâtricule Stoïque, sewing puppet costumes, trying to guess what Edward meant by such cryptic marginal notes as "Spirits of the swamp: insects: Loie Fuller sleeves" and "alligators have tails," and missing him intensely.

We presented *The White Canoe* in Cotuit in September. Jamie Wolf and I cobbled together a postcard, poster, and program, without the guidance of Edward's usual semi-legible calligraphic notes on a yellow page. Edward's good friends Herbert Senn and Helen Pond, brilliant set designers for the Opera Company of Boston and Cape Playhouse among others, created a stunning puppet stage with a roll-up swamp backdrop, topping three old wooden doors Edward had persuaded Herbert and Rick Jones to link into a facade. The still-homeless Center for the Arts borrowed Cotuit's Freedom Hall to stage *The White Canoe* as our memorial to our inimitable, irreplaceable collaborator and friend.

Theater on the Bay and the Heron Bistro

presents

HEADS WILL ROLL

An archivist entertainment
of words and music
enacted
presented by le Théâtricule Stoïque
revised and directed by Edward Gorey
with the participation of Eric Edwards.
Jill Erickson, Vincent Myette, Joe
Richards and Carol Verburg

Under Beneath the auspices posthumous
patronage of Trebonianus Gallus   TREBONIANUS GALLUS

late whatever.
Tea whatever

Where, When, and (to some extent) Why

The first Edward Gorey shows in Woods Hole and Provincetown were staged in summer, to catch the Cape's high tide of tourists and part-timers. At PAPA/PTC, a diverse, congenial group of fellow artists welcomed Edward not only into our performance space at the Provincetown Inn, but also our weekly Playwrights' Workshop, often followed by supper downtown, and occasionally some après-show revelry. It was a happy contrast to his solitary work of drawing and writing books.

Theatre sank its claws deeper into Edward when we moved to Bourne, a much shorter drive for him and also for his favorite Woods Hole actors. Why not a Christmas play? Wouldn't people welcome a change from (as reviewer Evan Albright put it) "watching a uniformed man with jaws as big as a tree mulcher fight a bunch of armed rats"? Once Edward broke the seasonal barrier (not that *Blithering Christmas* ousted *A Christmas Carol*), I suggested he try directing somebody else's work: Oscar Wilde? He picked *Salome*, produced by Jane Macdonald while I was in California.

Jane also made the first Cotuit connection. Working at the Cotuit Center for the Arts opened up all kinds of possibilities: for instance, my *Hamlet* had an original score composed by Jamie Wolf and performed by his music students, and a set designed by Edward and painted by other local artists. Jamie and his henchpeople encouraged us to try anything. Edward found the small space ideal for drama, dance, and music experiments with his hand puppets. Marionettes et al. didn't intrigue him so much; he was fascinated by the expressiveness of the human hand.

As fond as he was of drawing, writing, sewing, and watching TV at home with his cats, Edward flourished in good company. It's hard not to wonder how different things might be now if the Arts Center hadn't burned down just when he was putting off drastic action for his heart problem, awaiting the Easter arrival of half a dozen friends, the completed *White Canoe,* and a visit from the Tiger Lillies to discuss a collaboration. His last shocked phone call to me in San Francisco was about the fire–our artistic home, gone! We talked about doing a benefit when I got back.

Who and How

The ideal cast for a Gorey entertainment comprised four men and four women (to Edward, boys and girls), who played all the roles. If we couldn't find eight, six or seven would do. Naïveté charmed him; slickness irked him. In addition to his four core Upper Cape actors, a floating troupe of regulars developed, whose phone numbers I listed in my address book under F for FOE, "Friends of Edward": these were the first thespians I was to call for whatever theatrics he was up to. In some pieces he deployed them as actors, in others as puppeteers. Aside from those first three years in Provincetown, this "Aubergine Company" moved with him from venue to venue, and after a while he built his scripts with them in mind. The FOE were distinguished by bravery, imagination, and good nature as well as talent. This was fortunate, as for Edward loyalty tended to outweigh discrimination: Once you were cast in a show of his, you were automatically welcome in the next one.

His sets were as simple as his drawings for books were intricate. At the center stood a solid screen eight feet wide and six feet three inches high –just tall enough to hide the top of Eric Edwards's head. A narrow ledge along the top of the screen was the puppet stage. A table behind it held props. In front of the screen was the actors' stage, a performing space perhaps fifteen feet wide and ten feet deep. Around it Edward might arrange a few chairs, or a small picket fence, or some oversized fans and flowers. In Woods Hole, Bourne, and Cotuit, Phyllis Hartley usually carried out Edward's plans and helped him find missing pieces. The floor was almost always painted black; usually the background and screen were black, too, or occasionally white. For one entertainment he chose purple. Sometimes he would decorate the screen with plastic ivy or a painted design. For *Cautionary Tales,* his first show at the Cotuit Center for the Arts, the screen was a section of palisade fence. For *Useful Urns,* his first show with the Provincetown Theatre Company, he hand-painted six stunning black-and-white urns on styrofoam panels –again, just big enough to hide the actors–which (thanks to PAPA/PTC board member Butch Francis) had lightweight wooden feet to rest on and handles for the concealed actors to move them around.

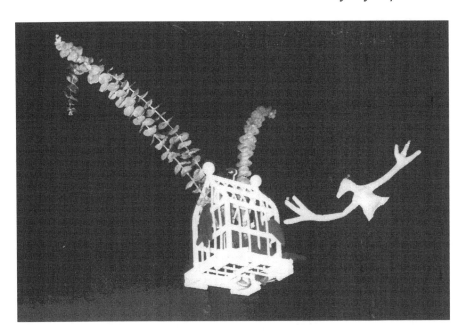

A typical entertainment (see pages 26-27) might feature actors in ten
pieces and puppets in four, with some overlap. Few pieces contained
much dialog; mostly they were narrated, by the participants in the
action or someone outside it or both. Some puppet skits had only
music. The dog dances to Beethoven's "Bagatelles" were unforgettable,
as were the puppet "Claire de Lune" and "Flower Duet" from *Lakme.*
Stuffed Elephants and *Useful Urns* featured original music by Paul Mascott;
for most of the other entertainments, Edward chose (and he or I taped)
classical and sometimes a few modern passages to play between scenes.

Mime was key, props arbitrary. In "The Helpless Doorknob," an actor
declaring "Angus concealed a lemon behind a cushion" was expected to
convey this act with neither a lemon nor a cushion. "The Deranged
Cousins," on the other hand, utilized a real brown glass doorknob and
bottle. Edward scoured yard sales for promising objects–less for
illustration than for provocative juxtaposition. Some would appear in
the actors' hands, others on the walls or screen. He learned that the
most dangerous, and also the most personally amusing, move he could
make was to give his actors any prop–balls of yarn, strings of beads,
bags of confetti–with the potential to spread beyond its scripted role.

Costumes for the entertainments were minimal–typically, a white shirt, white pants for the men and skirts for the women, and white canvas sneakers, plus whatever embellishments struck Edward's fancy, such as colored suspenders or Victorian fripperies. In a few shows, costumer Claudia Gray upgraded the fripperies with real antiques. For a finale, everyone might wear funny shoes or miner's lamps or whirl a Fourth-of-July sparkler. Costumes for the plays were more elaborate: in *Stumbling Christmas* (see page 30), each actor played three roles in a basic Edwardian dress or suit modified with garden hats, shawls, trenchcoats, pearls, and other accessories. In *Blithering Christmas*, Edward made a crocodile-tail train for Odile and a silver automaton outfit for Otto.

He also hand-sewed all 200-odd costumes for Le Théâtricule Stoïque, in stitching as precise as a machine's. These are three-fingered gloves: two of the actor's fingers sleeved in mitten-handed arms, one wiggled into a papier-mâché head. Most are cotton or cotton blends, in solid colors, plaids, and a wild variety of patterns. The *Omlet* gloves are muted shades of velvet, like the actors' costumes he chose for my *Hamlet*. Rosencrantz and Guildenstern is one gold glove with two heads. A few costumes have lace collars or tiny buttons. Two alligators are grass-green silk, down to their claws, and there's a black satin bat or two.

Male puppet heads look like small textured white eggs with the hint of a nose and tiny black dots for eyes. Female heads are the same except for a white bun on top. Edward's plastic box of puppet heads also included dogs, cats, alligators, and aberrations, along with rubber library thumbs to keep them from slipping off. They did anyway: hence the title *Heads Will Roll* for his first all-puppet show.

H E A D S W I L L R O L L
An Etceterist Entertainment
of words and music

devised & directed by Edward Gorey
enacted by the puppets of
Le Théâtricule Stoïque

with the participation of Eric Edwards, Jill Erickson, Vincent Myette,
and Joe Richards & Carol Verburg

M.B.L. Club, Water Street, Woods Hole

Thursday, July 18 and Friday, July 19 at 8 PM
to benefit Theater on the Bay
Suggested donation $8

For more information call 548-3705 x238

Productions generally ran for about a month, weekends only, three or four performances between Thursday and Sunday nights. Most of our theatres seated forty to a hundred, and the shows drew full enough houses to yield a nice profit for the venue. None of the participants got paid. Some audiences, and some reviewers, loved the plays; some were baffled, a few repelled. One night during *Chinese Gossip,* two tipsy men wandered in and tried to order takeaway. Fairly often Gorey fans would come backstage looking for Edward, seeking (or demanding) the same passionate attention from him that they gave his work. Gentleman that he was, Edward couldn't stand to be rude to people, even those who were rude to him. So part of my role was to steer away the more importunate or spooky ones when he wanted to focus on his show.

For every play or entertainment he created, Edward supplied original art for, and had made, most or all of the following: posters (photocopies for publicity, lithographs for sale), mugs, T-shirts, buttons, postcards, and the program cover. Usually he paid for the manufacturing and donated the proceeds to the venue, with some items held for Andreas Brown to sell through the Gotham Book Mart in New York. He also typed every script on a manual typewriter and brought in a bound copy for each cast and crew member (although sometimes we had to assemble them ourselves). He rarely altered dialogue once rehearsals started, but he frequently changed place names–either on the original in his trademark black calligraphic pen, or as verbal notes.

Direction

As a director, Edward's favorite maxim was that the director's job is to keep the actors from running into the furniture. He took great pleasure in watching nonprofessional actors and puppeteers figure out how to perform his work. Although he usually had an idea how he wanted a piece to look and move onstage, he left most of the details–including who should play which parts–up to the actors. As self-assigned stage manager, I wrote down the directions he and they hammered out, since otherwise Edward might well yield to the temptation to reconceive everything from scratch at the next rehearsal.

Not surprisingly, he scoffed at motivation and character development. "Just say the lines!" he would groan. Rarely were his criticisms harsher, or more specific, than "No no no no *no!*" or "Don't *act* so much." If an actor pressed him for help, he might turn the question over to me: "Ask Madame la directrice."

In refusing to give the actors any background for their roles or any emotions for their speeches, he also refused to tell the audience how they ought to react. Here his theatrical work mirrors his books. Edward took his responsibility to be simply to show what happened to whom; the audience was free to infer or impose whatever emotional response they saw fit.

This is not to say he didn't direct at all. If he wasn't satisfied with the shape a piece took, he tinkered with it, changing the actors' movements, timing, or props, sometimes right up through dress rehearsal. Once the show opened, he let it go. Although he might squelch the occasional hammy improvisation, generally the actors were free to "run amok"– and did, gleefully. Edward attended every performance, for the same reason he'd attended every performance of Balanchine's New York City Ballet: to watch the thing evolve, to catch the instants of inspiration, the actors' burgeoning confidence, courage, and experimentation. When something delighted him, he rewarded the perpetrator with a distinctive hooting laugh.

We all worked for that laugh. As we rehearsed *The White Canoe* after his death, our theatre felt unbearably empty without Edward's blue-jeaned, work-shirted figure and his whoop of a laugh. Even more, we missed the utterly unpredictable directorial flashes that made Edward's productions inimitable. "Here, you're all draped in scarves." "Augustus is a dog." "Hold up the colored plates like shop windows the tourist is looking into." "You come out carrying this." (A baby-shaped bundle of rags.) "Chuck it under the chin–coochie coochie! Then you look around, and you toss it over the screen."

ENGLISH SOUP

devised and directed by Edward Gorey

Act One
Overture
The Phthysical Xiphopagus
Ferry Tale I
With Love All Things are Possible
The Epiplectic Bicycle
Ferry Tale II
The Forgotten Trip
The Lawn Party

* * * * *
Fifteen-minute intermission
* * * * *

Act Two
Overture
The Doubtful Guest
Ferry Tale III
The Eggplant Frog
Horror at Hamstrung Hall
Litanies

CAST

Eric Edwards   Joe Richards
Jill Erickson   Cathy Smith
Jane Macdonald   Michael Ventura
Nicole Noel

and the puppets of Le Théâtricule Stoïque

* * * * *

Producer   Carol Verburg
Stage Manager   James Wolf

Music by Vivaldi, Ferdericks [sic], Muller,
Mozart, Rosser, and frogs

Dog by Barry Pinske

Ferry Tales from *Contes au bac* by Madame
Machine, englished by Mrs. Regera Dowdy

Special thanks to: Phyllis, PJ, & Atlas
Leigh, Arlene, & Cape Cod Travel
Dawn, Nicole, & Storyopolis

Following these performances *English Soup* will appear
Halloween weekend at Storyopolis in Los Angeles.

More from the Press: *Stumbling Christmas*

"Hellbent Hall, on the wilds of Mortshire, is bracing for a reunion of the Stumbling family. Separated by continents and disposition, the Stumblings, their servants, their cousins, friends and hangers-on are gathering for Christmas. "Stumbling Christmas," a new work written, directed and designed by Edward Gorey, reviews their past and present lives.

Hellbent Hall is being prepared for the holidays by Aunt Augusta, who is sewing new fringe on the draperies, and by Uncle Augustus, who is applying fresh gilt to the ballroom chairs. Butlers Kibble and Crouton and house manager Mrs. Forsooth are busy greeting the guests who arrive at the front door, each bringing a fruitcake.

Among the guests are Cousin Ripsley and Violet Gentian, both of whom are slightly off balance. They believe themselves to be spys and spend much of their time searching for other spys. Also arriving are Henrietta and George Toehold, cousins of the family, and Charlotte and James Stumbling, first cousins twice removed, who are secretly engaged."

– Melanie Bauer, *Sunday Cape Cod Times*, November 26, 1995

"Stumbling Christmas" requires a tremendous amount of concentration from its audience to keep up with the play's frenetic pace and convoluted storyline. Some 18 characters, portrayed by only five actors, weave in and out . . . Don't waste a lot of energy trying to keep the characters straight so that you can keep track of the plot. Mr. Gorey . . . flits from plot strand to plot strand and resolves not a one. . . .

What makes this play truly worth seeing are the characters outside the family. As P.G. Wodehouse proved in his series of stories about aristocrat Bertie Wooster and his butler, Jeeves, the hired help gets all the best lines. Cathy Smith's Mrs. Forsooth (she had been Miss Forsooth, governess to the Stumbling children, but out of respect for her years of service, the Stumblings promoted her to Mrs.) is a delightful ball of bubbling energy just as the two butlers, Kibble and Crouton (played by Joe Richards) are equally entertaining in their dour observations as they greet the incoming family members one by one. Best of all is Claudia Gray's Mrs. Uh, the Eliza Doolittle housekeeper with an attitude. . . .

By attempting to blend George S. Kaufman with Franz Kafka, Mr. Gorey's "Stumbling Christmas" presents an alternative to the usual pap thrown at audiences during the holiday season."

– Evan J. Albright, *Bourne Courier*, Thursday, Dec. 7, 1995

11314854R0002

Made in the USA
Lexington, KY
06 October 2011